CIVIL AND COMMERCIAL MEDIATION

CONTENTS

THANKS

PRESS

CHAPTER I

HISTORICAL EVENTS

CHAPTER II

TELEMATIC MEDIA,

TRIBUTE MEDIA,

CONSUMER ADR

CHAPTER III

CONCILIATION IN THE PURPOSE

COMMUNITY

CHAPTER IV

THE REFORM OF MEDIATION

CIVIL AND COMMERCIAL

CHAPTER V

CHARACTERISTICS OF MEDIATION

CHAPTER VI

MEDIA-QUESTION

CHAPTER VII

THE ROLE OF THE ADVOCATE,

THE PARTIES

THE MEDIATOR

CHAPTER VIII

MEDIA BODIES,

SECRETARY

EXPERTS

CHAPTER IX

DIFFERENCES WITH THE ARBITRO AND THE JUDGE,

DIFFERENCES

BETWEEN ASSISTED NEGOTIATION

AND CIVIL AND COMMERCIAL MEDIA

CHAPTER X

VERBAL TYPE

CHAPTER XI
COSTS, TIMES, FREE PATROCINE
COSTS
TIMES
FREE PATROCINO
CHAPTER XII
LEGISLATIVE DECREE 28/2010
D. M. 18 OCTOBER 2010 N.180
MINISTERIAL CIRCULATION
DECEMBER 20, 2011

BIBLIOGRAPHY

Acknowledgments

The idea of writing a book on mediation matured in April 2011, immediately after the justice reform came into force.
After taking a course as a professional mediator, I immediately realized that it was an evolving subject, as it was different from the typical patterns of the legal landscape.

I also noticed, that it was not known by many people, as a way of resolving conflicts, and in the face of a controversy the ordinary road was always preferred, with non-programmable temporal consequences.

So I started looking for material to write a book.

I analyzed the ADR system with a watchful eye to current regulations, which are constantly evolving.

It was a nice journey that I traveled with great joy.

I thank and dedicate this book to all the people who in my life have supported and esteemed me in the past, they do it in the present and they will do it in the future.

Vitale Rosalba

PREMISE

Conciliation can be defined as an alternative method (A.D.R. - Alternative Disputure Solution) conflicts, according to which a third impartial person, the conciliator, assisting parties by guiding their negotiation and orienting them towards seeking mutual agreements satisfactory.

With the initials A.D.R. all methods are identified alternative dispute resolution (Mediation, conciliation, arbitration) that have the advantage of allowing fast and effective resolution of litigation, reducing the excessive judicial burden and without however, they become an obstacle to access to justice ordinary.

Common features of ADRs are those to manage controversies with simplified techniques and contained in the time and cost, based on specific competencies and therefore more appropriate to the social context, by favoring the restoring interpersonal and commercial relationships[1].

---

[1] 1 (E. SEVERIN What Place Is there for Civil Mediation in Europe ?, in G.ALPA, R. DANOVI (edited by), The out-of-court resolution of disputes and the role of the lawyer, Milan, 2004).

ADR techniques are not alternative to justice, but represent, a mode of social regulation that is alongside the right to disputes[2].

The alternative to the normal means of award is puts in the fact that no reason or petty is attributed to it does it right, but one of the parties in conflict is one compositional vision of the conflict.

They are fully in the context of policies aimed at improving access to justice playing a role complementary and not simply alternative to the proceedings as they allow the parties to establish a dialogue, which would otherwise be impossible to achieve, leaving them at the same time free to evaluate on the possibility of resorting to traditional systems.

In the types of ADR third parties (mediation, conciliation, negotiation) do not make decisions, and the parties do approach to achieving a common purpose saddisfactory for both.

In the current law, the matter of conciliation comes first introduced with D.lgs. 5/2003 which governs it

---

[2] (C. Trouble, Private Autonomy and Conflict Management, Naples, 2007).

the application regarding corporate law, for then be treated completely in D.lgs. 28/2010.

CHAPTER I

BACKGROUND

The Adr method has very ancient origins, it can be traced in the ancient Rome of the fifth century BC.

In the first of the XII Tables describing the process of proposing and dealing with an action judicial, it was stated, that: "Rem ubi pacunt, greedy. Ni pacunt, in comitio aut in foro ante meridiem caussam coicide ", that is, whether the parties in dispute had an agreement (pactio) then the judge would have been obliged to consecrate him with the issuance of a judgment while in the case of If there was no agreement, then the judicial channels would be brought establishing process[3].

An agreement that was made with the intervention of old people essays recognized by the associates who helped resolve litigation.

---

[3] books.google.com/books?isbn=8838756333

In that era an estimated pacifier figure was one Roman Consul of 503 BC by the name Agrippa Menenio Wooled.

The Consul called for the fight between patricians and plebeians in 494 BC, in secession on the Sacred Mountain, he succeeded sedate it with a metaphor.

He sets the social order to the body human being declaring that: << if all parts of the body

they collaborate, it survives, if the parties disagree among them, all parts perish >> [4].

("Olim human artus, cum ventrem otiosum cernerent, ab and discordarunt, conspiraruntque ne manus ad os cibum ferent, nec os acciperent datum, nec dentes conficerent. Acts dum ventrem tomare volunt, ipsi quoque defecerunt, totumque corpus ad extremam tabem venit: inde apparition ventris haud signs ministerium esse, eumque acceptos cibos for omnia limbs dissere, et cum and o in gratiam redierunt. As senatus et populous almost unum corpus discord pereunt concordia valent ") [5].

---

[4] www.m.wikipendia.org/wiki/Agrippameneniolanato/en

[5] Tito livio, ab urbe dresses books, VIII, 33

In Greece were the Aralds called the "conservatives of peace" who maintained friendships with peoples foreigners or enemies.

Subjects of inconceivable moral conduct were elected by community and were held in great consideration for the orality of the words with which they declared war or they played the games.

The sign of their public office was a stick similar to the sacred caduceus of the Greek god Hermes, symbolizing the conciliation between two opposites, creation of harmony between different elements, such as water, fire, earth and air[6].

In the East, the Confucius doctrine based on Harmony interior, triggered in the population the idea of moving away any form of conflict with the voluntary search of one compromise solution without having to sue.

In the Middle Ages it was the Church to act as a mediator between associates, between the Kingdoms and Principals and the City State, by performing also judicial functions in the Ecclesiastical Courts[7].

---

[6] https://it.wikipedia.org/wiki/Araldo

[7] www.wikipedia.org

The Indians of America used to solve the issues tribal sums, how to decide peace or war through a council consisting of elders or bosses.

Board members were chosen as tribal leaders by all the adults of the community. Every decision was made to unanimity. Personal conflicts were solved through the mediation of the tribal leader or a family member[8].

Even in the United States of America mediation is mainly stated in the form of consulting services and reconciliation within the courts.

In Europe, the French Revolution affirmed the juge de paix, who had the task of maintaining peace between them associates.

The juge de paix was not a lawyer but a subject voted by the community to be distinguished for high dignity morality and social status[9].

---

[8] www.libertarianation.org/2013/01/23/la-societa-senza-stato-degli-indianidamerica

[9] www.fr.wikipedia.org/wiki/Justice_de_paix_en_France

This figure was brought to Italy by the armed forces Napoleonic and, with the years, then made mandatory with the Civil Procedure Code from 1865 to one international regulation through the directive n. 2008/52 / EC of the European Parliament and of the Council of May 21, 2008.

The purpose of the Directive was to facilitate the use of mediation through the establishment of a Community

common minimum legislation relative to a certain one number of common elements in the civil procedure[10].

Subsequently, its adoption was carried out further work.

In 2010, the Italian government issued the D.lgs. March 4, 2010, n. 28 dictating a homogeneous discipline in the ADR sector[11].

In 2012 the Justice Program was launched, the 2013/11 / EU Directive for Consumers ADR11 and

---

[10] www.newsmercati.com

[11] OJ L 165, 18.6.2013, p. 63

the EU Regulation no. 524/2013 on the Resolution of online consumer disputes[12].

An online platform with a European reach online transaction object between consumers and professionals.

In 2013 with the Decree Law of June 21, 2013, n. 69 "Decree of making", converted with modifications by law August 9, 2013, n. 98, the Government has made changes to D.lgs 28/2010 proposing mediation as the legality of the proceedings trying to cleanse it from unconstitutionality profiles taken by the Court (Article 84).

In the new regulatory dictation the "Delegated mediation" in which the court appealed can arrange for reconciliation, assistance obligatory of the lawyer, duration of the proceedings reduced to 3 months, and in case of failure to attend mediation, to the senses of the art. 116, paragraph 2, cf., p condemnation of the party who did not participate in the payment at the entrance of the state budget of a

---

[12] OJ L 165, 18.6.2013, p. 1

sum of amount corresponding to the unified contribution due for the judgment.

CHAPTER II

TELEMATIC MEDIA, MEDIATION TRIBUTE, ADR CONSUMERS

1. TELEMATIC MEDIA

The procedure can be implemented with the agreement of the parties.

Online mediation is always allowed in cases where a party participates in videoconferencing and the other, with prior consent, physically participate in the presence of the mediator at the seat of the Organization.

The requirements are:

- own a fixed computer or notebook connected to the internet and equipped with webcam, microphone and headphones / audio speakers;

- parties to use the telematic service must register on the website of the mediation body in the form of data acquisition, which once verified by the system, to which you are presenting the mediation application, which must be printed, signed and sent to the secretariat of the Organization with attached copies of the document of approval of the petitioner and a copy of the proof of payment of the costs of initiating the procedure.

The secretariat of the body will then, if necessary, contact the other party who, in the event of adherence to the procedure, will also carry out registration at the telematic mediation platform (possibly assisted by the secretariat of the body) and the filing of the documentation.

- parties participate in mediation through videoconferencing, directly from their home or studio;

- parts (users and mediator) can talk in real time at a distance;

- if the user is not able to access telematically by himself, he / she may (with the consent of the other party) go to the headquarters of the Organization and liaise with the help of a representative of the Organization;

- at the end of the meeting, the parties will be able to receive a copy of the minutes certifying the terms and conditions of the agreement reached, in electronic form, via the certified electronic mail circuit (and, eventually, at their home address) lack of agreement;

- the subscription of the minutes can take place both in digital (digital signature) mode and in analogue mode (autographed signature).

- in the event of digital signature unavailability, the minutes and agreements must be signed during the videoconference meeting and telematically sent by the mediator to the parties, who are responsible for printing to subscribe and authenticate the signatures to an official public.

The parties then send the paperwork documentation to the mediator that verifies the correspondence of verbs and agreements authenticated with those signed in videoconferencing.

- pursuant to the third paragraph of art. 11, D.lgs 4/3/2010 n. 28, in the event that the parties make one of the acts referred to in art. 2643 cc, the signing of the minutes must be "authenticated by an authorized public officer".

2. TRIBUTE MEDITATION

The institute of tax mediation has been introduced from article 39, paragraph 9, of dl 98/2011 which he inserted in Legislative Decree 546/1992, Article 17-bis, entitled "The Complaint and mediation."

The law has entered the Italian system for the controversies worth no more than fifty thousand euros, relating to the acts of the Revenue Agency, notified to with effect from 1 April 2012 and for acts issued by Enti (Municipalities, Customs and Equitalia), a remedy to be tried out whenever an appeal is sought to the Tax Commission. "Authenticated by an authorized public officer".

In particular, the acts concerned are: Notice of liquidation, notice of assessment, a measure that removes sanctions, role, refusal expressed or tacit of the restitution of taxes, sanctions money and interest or other unpaid accessories, denial or withdrawal of leniency or denial of applications easy definition of tax relations, any other act issued by the revenue agency, for which the law provides for the plaintiff to stand alone tributary commissions, property and property classes allocation of cadastral rent, in the measure of compatibility in case of faults of the folder of payment or appeal of the hold of registered goods or mExcludes acts: Of a value higher than twenty thousand euros, of indeterminate value, concerning activities of the recovery agent, relating to non-acts which is not passively legitimate the revenue office, of acts notified before 1 April 2012, of tacit repayment waste with reference to which on April 1, 2012 (November 30, 2012 for the requests submitted to the offices of the former agency of the territory) have already been 90 days from the presentation of the application for repayment, concerning recovery of State aid, of measures issued pursuant to Article 21 ("sanctions accessory ") of Legislative Decree no. 472 of acts relating to the cases referred to in Article 22ortgage registration. ("Mortgage and custodial sequestration") of D.lgs. n. 472 of 1997, of the denial of the closure of "minor" tax disputes pending provisions of Article 39, paragraph 12 of Decree no. 98 of 2011. The benefits that derive from tax mediation mainly are:

(a) the reduction of administrative penalties of 60% a benefit that can be recognized even if the taxpayer decides to pay the tax entirely mediation process.

The mediation agreement ends with the subscription by the office and the taxpayer and perfect with the payment within twenty days of the full amount due or the first installment, in the case of a payment in one up to eight quarterly installments of equal amount.

Payment must be made with the f24 model. In case of non - payment of the installments after the First, the act of mediation constitutes the title for the compulsory collection that legitimizes the tax authority a to place the residual sums due and the sanctions of the 60% on the residual amount.

The same rule applies to the taxpayer, the which can act before the ordinary magistrate in the end to obtain an injunction if the body does not give execution to payment.

Conversely, in the event of a failure to agree, the eventual subsequent tax judgment, costs of judgment, not are increased by 50% but interest is due the failure to perfect mediation.

The application is not subject to the stamp duty and must be notified to the regional or provincial or to the operational center the competent revenue agency or the office provincial - territory that issued the act, with the the manner and the deadline for the appeal.

Nine days after receipt of the instance from part of the Regional or Provincial or Center Directorate operational or provincial office – territory without the mediation being concluded or that the acceptance, even partial, has taken place, or the denial of the instance, begins after the end of thirty days for the eventual constitution of the taxpayer, to whom the employee's suspension is applied of the terms.

The constitution takes place with the deposit at the provincial tax commission, appeal with the instance.

If the taxpayer receives the denial or acceptance partial by the nineteenth day, the term for the eventual constitution starts from the date of receipt.

Recently, Law no. 147/2013 stipulated that the a claim is a matter of lawfulness of the action.

b) in accordance with dl 35/2013 the taxpayer may compensate unsecured, certain, liquid and debit credits, vested in the comparisons of the public administrations indicated in Article 1, paragraph 2 of Legislative Decree 165/2001, for deliveries and contracts, with the sums owed following adherence assessment, adherence to the invitation to the contradiction or the verbal record of finding, acquiescence, simplified definition of sanctions, judicial conciliation and mediation.

In this regard, the Constitutional Court, in its judgment of 16 April 2014, n. 98 considered these remedies to be resolved of disputes satisfy the general interest under two aspects:

Saves time and cost, and reduces litigation before tax tribunals.

Therefore, the taxpayer before resorting to the Provincial Tax Commission addresses to the Agency of the Revenue, a claim, to apply for the annulment partial or total, including a proposal in the instance of mediation.

As of March 2, 2014, the term for constitution the parties 'proceedings take effect from the end of the

90' s days from the receipt of the instance by the office.

In case of filing the appeal before the end of this term, the revenue agency may appeal the impracticability of the appeal by postponing the discussion to mediation.

With the 2014 Stability Law, two were added provisions:

1) The sums due as social security contributions and welfare benefits do not apply sanctions and interests.

2) The presentation of the instance involves the suspension of the execution of the act held for 90 days. However, the taxpayer or the tax authority may to make progress on the judgment instituted by the Provincial Tax Commission for Composition of the lite.

The initiative may be initiated by the parties or by the Commission tributary that the parties will be able to subscribe by subscribing to hearing, conciliation report.

If the agreement is not reached, the Commission Taxation sets a deadline for the parties to agree postponing the hearing no later than 60 days.

The minutes signed at the hearing constitute the title for the collection on the basis of the dispute settlement.

Within 20 days of notification of the canceled order matter of the dispute filed by the committee taxpayer, the taxpayer pays the full amount taxes and accessories, or the first installment of the same in the event that it has been granted, afterwards explicit request, the payment of the tax charge which can not exceed 8 quarterly rates.

3. ADR CONSUMERS

Legislative Decree no. 130/2015 published in G.U. on 19 August 2015, n. 191 has implemented Directive 2013/11 / EU of Parliament and the European Council beginning with alternative and out-of-court resolution procedure (alternative dispute resolution) for litigation between the through the establishment of a platform web as well as locating entities that manage them procedures.

In particular, the provisions of the decree apply to the voluntary redistribution procedures for the resolution, even telematic, of "national" disputes and cross-border ", between consumers (ie all citizens private individuals) and "professionals" (ie suppliers of goods and services according to the Consumer Code) resident and established in the European Union.

According to art. 141- octies of consumer code I Organizations interested in it may apply for be included in a list kept by an authority specially invested in this task (Ministero della Justice, together with the Ministry of Development economic, in relation to the Register of Organizations of consumer mediation, Consob, authorities for electricity, gas and water systems, Agcom, Bank of Italy).

The Ministry of Economic Development looks after the list dividing it into two sections.

- Bodies operating through joint negotiations ex art. 141-ter for sectors where there is no authority independent regulation and for those in which, albeit there is an authority to regulate it, it does not have it specifically adopted and applied specific provisions relative to the inscription of this type of organisms, and therefore in the latter case only transiently up to the application of any such regulatory provisions (Joint Conciliation Body Consortium Netcomm - Consumer Associations, Organization of parity conciliation Trenitalia S.p.a., Organization of joint conciliation Poste Italiane S.p.a.

- Organizations formed by Chambers of Commerce to the senses of the art. 2, paragraph 2, letter g) and paragraph 4 of the law 29 December 1993 n. 580, limited to disputes between consumers and professionals, do not return to the register of Consumer mediation bodies of cui to the art. 16, paragraphs 2 and 4 of Legislative Decree 4 March 2010, no. 28 (CCIAA of Naples, CCIAA of Cosenza, conciliation desk of the Milan- Online Service)[13].

The dispute ends within 90 days of the proposal for mediation application, term which can be extended for another 90 days due to particular causes complex.

---

[13] www.sviluppoeconomico.gov.it

The procedure is free or at a minimum without being obliged to be defended by a lawyer.

In disputes concerning the supply of electricity or gas, after the first level complaint is expected, in the event of a failure, an attempt to compulsory conciliation in front of the Service of Conciliation of the AEG, or in front of the Organizations of Out-of-court settlement of disputes referred to in the Resolution 209 of 5 May 2016 of the AEEG itself.

By order of 25 May 2017 the Court of First Instance Rome, he pointed out, that this compulsory attempt must to be considered applicable only to disputes that are end users or users to introduce to them operators and operators.

The conciliation procedure with the AEEG "is active in the event of a failure or unsatisfactory response to the complaint of first level "and that such complaint is only possible by the end customers and prosumer and not by operators and gestori[14].

---

[14] Tribunal of Rome text order 24-25 May 2017

It should also be noted that the judgment no. 7090/2017 of 22 June 2017, with which the Milan Tribunal established, that in matters of contingency between telephone companies and a user to recover a credit they have controversial, it is necessary to experience in the penalty of impropriety, a preventive attempt to conciliate before the Corecom competent for territory.

CHAPTER III

MEDIATION

IN THE COMMUNITY

At Community level the main references regulatory requirements for ADR are:

- Recommendation 98/257 / EC of 30 March 1998 concerning the principles applicable to organs responsible for extrajudicial resolution of the consumer disputes;

- Recommendation 2001/310 / EC of 4 April 2001 concerning the principles applicable to organs out-judges participating in the resolution consensual disputes over the consumption;

- Resolution of May 25, 2000 "E And J-Net" of the Council on a Community network of bodies for the extra-judicial resolution of the consumer disputes;

- Directive 2000/31 / EC of 8 June 2000 European Parliament and Council on certain legal aspects of the company's services of the information, in particular the trade electronic commerce, in the internal market;

- Resolution of the European Parliament of 25 April of 2001 (A5-0134 / 2001) on the action taken in on Community policy on the out of court settlement of disputes in consumer goods;

- Green Paper of 19 April 2002.

- Directive 2008/52 / EC.

This last legislation calls on states to guarantee them consumers access to Adr to resolve conflicts national and trans-national.

Specifically, the minimum common content that all Countries must respect are:

- the consumer must try before activating one ADR procedure a direct, bilateral resolution of its own dispute through an adequate one complaints system (to which, however, the directive does not applies pursuant to art. 2, paragraph 2, lett. (e) to which will follow pursuant to art. Article 5 (4) of the Directive, access to the ADR system conditioned by the Advice to the professional.

- the mediation bodies will have to conclude the procedure by a decision within 90 days from the moment it received the complete dossier of the complaint except for the hypothesis of procedures particularly complex.

- keep confidentiality on the cases handled though will be able to publish exemple decisions on controversies of particular importance "so facilitate the exchange of information and best practices concerning consumer rights in the sectors specific. " obligation to inform the parties of the consequences of choices in the context of the ADR procedure.

- Using the Adr system in a free or small way expensive for consumers[15].

- Member States shall ensure, where the parties so wish they choose mediation, not to prevent the launch of a judicial or arbitration proceedings in relation to the dispute if during the proceedings of mediation has expired the prescription or decadenza[16]. So much so, it is worth analyzing how

---

[15] www.dirittoegiustizia.it/.../L_Europa_detta_le_nuove_rego le_sui_sistemi di_ADR_su ...

[16] G.AUTORINO STAZIONE, ADR general profiles, www.comparazionedirittocivile.it

they are you have transposed these provisions in different countries.

In Austria: Mediation is a paid service. The mediators are registered in the register maintained by Minister of Justice after attending a course in training. There is no code of ethics or regulation specific;

Mediation is used to solve any civil law dispute. The agreement has executive force, if it is formalized by a notary or a civil court.

In Switzerland: The mediation procedure is free. The mediator is paid on an hourly or daily basis to be agreed with the parties at the beginning of the mediation.

The injured party can file a petition with the Civil Chambers of the Court of Appeal for disputes arising in the context of a public or private employment relationship.

England and Wales: The Ministry of Justice promotes policy specificities in mediation identifiable in two main organs: the Civil Mediation Council and Family Mediation Council.

The procedure is handled voluntarily. Mediators are not required to comply with a code specification.

The parties that have, reached an agreement can turn to the judge for this, after having approved the agreement will turn it into a measure binding order.

In Scotland: The Mediation Agency takes the name of Legal System Division, Constitution, Law and Courts Directorate and is responsible for all of them mediation policies.

Mediation is provided for all areas of law and it is optional.

There is a general Scottish Registry of mediation (Scottish Mediation Register, SMR) that provides directions on how to find a mediator in Scotland. All brokers are required to comply with a code deontological and follow the programs of training for different sectors of mediation lasting at least 30 hours.

The cost of mediation is not governed by the state even if it is usually a free procedure in the case where it affects minorities.

The agreement reached becomes enforceable after having made available to the competent authorities.

In Northern Ireland: there is a resolution service of disputes called "Law Society of Northern Which establishes rules and procedures for the discipline of mediation services.

This institution is invoked to settle disputes even during the course of the process, both at the request of the parties and on the order of the Judge. It consists of a solicitor's college (attorneys) and barrister (lawyers) formats specifically through the courses to carry out the mediator function.

However, there are other organizations that do they deal with mediation like those of volunteering which take the name of Barnardos and Relate and of work by the Labor Relations Agency. Mediation operates predominantly in the field civil and commercial.

The mediator's remuneration is left to the agreement of the parties[17].

The agreement reached and signed by both parties acquire the same value as a ruling.

In Belgium: mediation operates in civil matters, commercial, business and is managed in good shape voluntary.

Mediation centers known for issues commercial, are the "Business Mediation Center" of Brussels and the "Cepani", a national body, intersectoral and independent, composed of managers, business lawyers, lawyers and university professors, which performs several functions.

There is, for mediators, a disciplinary code mentioned "Code of good conduct". The authority responsible for checks is the Commission federal mediation that monitors periodic activity and update the list of mediators enabled.

---

[17] www.stelviopietrobono.it/index.php? ... mediation ... ireland-north ...

Enabling the profession to be exercised presupposes that the aspiring mediators carry out specific courses articulated in a common part of 60 hours divided into at least 25 hours of theoretical training and others 25 of practical training.

Then there are specific mediation programs in the civil, commercial and commercial law sectors social as well as refresher courses. The agreement signed by the parties is equated to a sentence; alternatively the homologation is possible transcription by a notarial act.

The Ombudsman's fees are agreed between the mediator and parties.

It is possible under the Community directive request the forced execution of a written agreement that results from a mediation. According to Articles 1733 and 1736 of the Judicial Code the mediation agreement can be approved by part of a judge who makes him executive.

In Finland: Mediation is used in both civil cases, both in criminal cases.

In civil mediation, all parties pay the sum which competes, while in criminal cases the service is free.

Substantial subjects can apply for patronage at the expense of the state at an office of legal assistance.

The mediator may be a third party or, if required by the parties, even a court judge.

The provincial offices of the national health service guarantee the availability of mediation services as well as their proper implementation throughout the country national court mediation services are managed by district courts.

There is no mandatory assistance from the lawyer and the formation of mediators is left all 'organizzazione del Terveyden ja hyvinvoinnin (THL).

Directive No. 2008/52 / EC allows the parties to ask for the content of a written agreement resulting from a mediation being rendered enforceable.

In France: parties can use the instrument of mediation in all areas of law. In the order no. 2011 - 1540 of November 16 you can read, if the parts were in front of the court, the court may, with the prior consent of the parties, appoint a third person for the parties parties compare their points of view and find a solution to the dispute (Article 131-1 of the Code of Civil Procedure).

The judge may also always impose on the parties, in specific cases such as parental or juvenile powers provisional measures concerning divorce, of take part in an informative meeting on mediation, which is free (Articles 255 and 373-2-10 of the Civil Code). It adds that it does not exist at national level or as one deontological code of mediators or a website related to mediation.

There is a great organization that takes its name of Fédération Nationale des Centres de Médiation (FNCM) and other private organizations with their own deontological codes.

There is no specific training for Exercise the profession of mediator, except of the family sector.

The FNCM which includes 61 mediation centers of forensic orders in which thousands of thousands are entered mediators require some requirements to be able to perform the profession of mediator consist of:

- 200 hours training divided into 40 hours base and 160 hours of insights.

- in 100 hours specialization courses in family and enterprise and training obligation 20 hours per year.

While in the family business, the decree December 2, 2003 and the Order of 12 February 2004, have specific training is provided by institutions recognized by the Regional Business Department health and social services (DRASS, Direction régionale des affaires sanitaires et sociales) and the release of a family mediation diploma by the Prefect of the region. Out-of-court or judicial mediation is not free and is not mandatory of the lawyer.

In the field of judicial mediation, the remuneration of the mediator comes under patronage at the expense of the state. In any case, it is fixed by the responsible magistrate taxation after the execution of the assignment and behind submission of a memorandum or a statement of expenditure (Article 119 of Decree No 91-1266 of 19 December 1991).

Parties undertake to pay a deposit in at the beginning of the procedure, the fee is paid to the mediator at the end of the procedure. For "family mediation" there is a tariff national variable according to party income.

The mediation agreement arising from the will of the parties are subject to the approval of the judge who he would have been in charge of the controversy. In case the agreement is part of a procedure judicial procedure, Article 131-12 of the Code of Procedure civil law provides that the court seised proceeds on the basis of an application by the same parties. Article L.111-3 1 ° of the Code of Civil Procedure of execution imply that they constitute securities executing the agreements resulting from mediation judicial or extrajudicial jurisdiction to which the jurisdictions judicial or administrative power conferred strength executive.

With a recent decree n. 2012- 66 of January 20th 2012, entered into force on January 23, 2012 was inserted in the Code of Civil Procedure a new book Including several articles devoted to the mediazione[18].

---

[18] https://www.adrintesa.it/wp.../LA-MEDIAZIONE-IN-FRANCIA-avv.- Guido-Cardelli.pdf

In Portugal: a state agency that deals with mediation is the GRAL (Gabinete para a Resolução Alternativa de Litigios).

GRAL imposes certain requirements on mediators to be enrolled, authorizes the courses held by private institutions that are also empowered to release accreditation in favor of participating mediators. The formation of mediators is guaranteed by private institutions. There is no Mediator Code of Conduct a national level, but the mediators exert their own activities in compliance with the European Code of Conduct.

The use of mediation is allowed in some areas, in particular for family and work issues and criminal law. Mediation can be both voluntary and delegated by the judge. In the first case, the costs of mediation are a loads of parts, except in the case of difficulty economically mature the right to exonerate submitting the application for legal aid at the expense of State.

And mediation delegated by the judge with the value of judgment is not subject to costs.

Legal assistance is not mandatory. In Romania: mediation is regulated by civil procedure code and deals with civil matters, commercial, family, criminal and the protection of the consumers.

Article. 109 c.p.c, states, that in reports commercials where there are controversies, before resort to the court must be done beforehand resort to direct conciliation. The applicant meets with the opposite party he shall inform the court in writing of the questions he has asked will deal with it. The real meeting of conciliation takes place lasted 15 days. Conciliation is formalized in a document written. Another form envisaged by the legislator is the mediation delegated by the judge. In such a case the judge in the process it recommends mediation to the parties, and these they agree to submit to the information session held by the mediator. Following the information session the parties will decide whether or not to participate in the procedure for resolve their dispute.

Within the deadline set by the judge (15 days) the parties they must present the report prepared by the mediator about the result of the information session. If the agreement between the parties intervenes this is transposed by the judge who becomes irrevocable and executive. The agreement is also enforced by means of one notary. And a contracted mediation is also possible.

The Romanian mediator is a subject capable of acting, graduate, with a working experience of at least 3 years, clinically fit, with a good reputation and that he was not definitively condemned for one a crime susceptible to affect the prestige of the mediator profession. You must also have completed a training course mediators or a postgraduate master, that is accredited in accordance with the laws and approved by Mediation Council (Consiliul de Mediere)[19].

---

[19] Art. 8 c. 3 l. 192/06. The Consiliul de Mediere is an autonomous entity public interest based in Bucharest. It consists of 9 members who may also be authorized mediators (Article 17). It stands by the exact fees for granting mediator permissions (Article 21). Has plurime skills: a) promote mediation and represent the interests of authorized mediators, to ensure the quality of services in the mediation field in accordance with the provisions of the law 192/06; b) elaborate training standards on mediation, on The mediator to carry out the profession must be authorized, under the

conditions provided for by law 192/06 and the authorization involves payment of a fee. The formation of mediators is left to private entities, the latter shall be subject to the authorization of Consiliul de Mediere. At present there is a training program valid as an initial course for 80 hours mediators. the basis of best international practice; c) authorize services / programs of continuous professional training, as well as those for the mediation specialization; d) prepare and update the list of training organizations that have obtained the authorization; is) to authorize the mediators, with respect to l. 192/06; and 1) cooperate with the competent authorities of other Member States of the European Union, of the The European Economic Community and the Swiss Confederation, so ensure the control of mediators and the services they provide, in compliance with the provisions of Government Urgent Decree no. 49/2009; f) prepare and update the group of authorized mediators; g) to have / maintain a clear picture of the structures of authorized mediators; h) vigilance on compliance with training standards for mediation; the) to issue documents attesting to the professional qualification of brokers; j) adopt the Code of Ethics (this was done in 2007) and professional mediators and the rules of liability specifications; k) adopt measures for compliance with the Code of Ethics and professional and apply disciplinary disciplinary rules same; l) elaborate proposals on mediation to modify the legislation in this field; m) adopt the regulations on the organization and the operation; n) organize the election of the next Council of

The law governs the organization of the activity of mediation.

The mediation office consists of at least 2 mediators and translators, lawyers can be hired or other specialized staff, as well as staff administrative and auxiliary.

Any authorized mediator may then hold one register, archive and own account.

They can participate in national and international associations to protect their profession and the own statute.

The remuneration is proportionate to nature and object of mediation[20].

In Hungary: mediation is managed by the ministry of justice with an ad hoc law issued in 2002, and with a log containing the names of the professional brokers and companies for which they work.

---

mediation, according to the law; o) meet any other skills, as indicated by law. (See Article 20 of 192/06).

[20] https://mediaresenzaconfini.files.wordpress.com/2012/01/strumenti-dicomposizione- conflict-of-in-romania.pdf

There is no mediator code of conduct with the only exception to the job title "Conciliation and Mediation Service in Causes del lavoro "(Labor Mediator and Arbitrator SZOLGÁLAT). Generally, brokers refer to the Code of Conduct European conduct. The use of mediation is voluntary and is a payment being the agreed broker's fee Between the parts. The mediation agreement can be enforced following the particular procedure provided by the European Community Directive, the number 2008/52 / EC.

In Malta: in 2004 the Maltese Center was set up for mediation.

It is an independent body with its own legal personality, which has the function of:

a) promote mediation as a means of national and international resolution.

(b) provide the appropriate structures for the holding of the procedures.

c) establish the criteria for the appointment of mediators and the list of mediators.

d) to approve the appointment of mediators.

e) keep the register of mediations and provide the custody of mediation documents.

f) to remove mediators in cases of incapacity or conflict of interest.

g) establish the ethical code that mediators have to to observe during the mediation process.

h) determine the fare to be paid for the services provided from the centre.

(i) facilitating access to the mediation procedure through the publication of information, lines guide and related documentation.

(l) draw up and publish an annual report on it progress of the Center.

m) advise or make recommendations to Minister on every issue that, in the opinion of the Board of Directors, may be of interest Ministerial.

n) carry out the statutory functions. The president of the Center must be a judge or a judge attorney with at least twelve years of experience. The vice president is a lawyer with the same experience. The Mediation Center is exonerated by each liability for the payment of taxes and VAT stamp duty. The use of mediation is voluntary and is left open to the free determination of the awarding authority about the running time of the whole procedure. Every mediation party can be assisted by one consultant, but if the mediation request comes by a decree of the civil or judicial authority commercial service may be solicited only lawyer. Mediation applies to civil law, of family, industrial and social security, and it is not free.

In Cyprus: there is no mediation body but a Cyprus Mediation Association. The mediators' association has entered into an agreement of collaboration in mediation with the Norway and Turkey and in this regard it is based on the Norwegian model for conflict resolution. Mediation is voluntary and the agreement does not Executive Effectiveness. Mediation is mandatory for the disputes of the work and is governed by the Code of Conduct industrial. Mediators in this area are government officials qualified and their training is entrusted to one private organizations.

In Greece: the use of mediation is optional and applies to matters pertaining to the law of work and commercial law. The mediator must be an accredited lawyer, except for cross-border disputes whose choice is free. Law no. 3898/2010 states that the Bodies of training are non-profit entities formed by one Advocates Advice and one or more Chambers of Commerce, authorized by the Department of the Ministry of Justice in charge[21].

The Agreement is signed by the Ombudsman and the parties Lawyers.

At the request of at least one of the parties, the mediator guarantees the filing of the original verbal in the secretariat of the court of first instance of the region where the mediation took place payment of the fee to the mediator. That verb is an executive order of which Article 904 (2) (c) of the Code of Conduct civil procedure.

In Germany: July 26, 2012 came into force in Germany the law on mediation (Mediationsgesetz).

---

[21]https://mediaresenzaconfini.org/2012/01/30/la-mediazione-in-pillolegrecia/

The law also indicates the scope of application of mediation (civil and commercial causes transnational also family law, the successions) introduced in the Civil Procedure Code German, incentives to promote the use of mediation. It enshrines the obligation for the parties that intend to promote action before the declare whether or not they have been provided make a preliminary attempt at resolution out of court, in the absence of the as the court can ask the grounds and propose it holding a mediation suspending the judgment until the full experiment of the attempt.

To do the mediator profession are not required special study titles such as degree or diploma. Training and updating are left out however to private organizations in the respect of the regulations issued by the Federal Ministry of Justice Justice. The fees of the professional broker are agreed from the same with the interested parties, the hourly cost it is normally between 80 and 250 euros. The agreement may be reached by mediation may become enforceable in case of intervention in mediation of a lawyer or notary[22].

In the Czech Republic: the Ministry of Justice is responsible for mediation and mediation surveillance of freely conditioned persons criminal matter.

In civil matters the mediation service is managed from the Association of Mediators of the Republic Czech, non-governmental body member of the Forum international mediation, equipped with a code of conduct. The use of mediation is permitted within the scope of the family law and commercial law. This is an optional and free procedure.

The Czech mediator has a master in mediation and must be registered with the Ministry. The judge may order the parties to turn to one mediator enrolled in the brokers' list for one lasting up to three hours and suspending within this period the relative procedure. The mediation agreement can be enforced in

---

[22]https://www.ar-net.it/news/la-mediazione-in-germania/

accordance with Community Directive 2008/52 / EC.

In Poland: In the Code of Civil Procedure of 28 July 2005 has been included in Chapter I, Section I, entitled "Mediation".

Since then, it has been regulated by the matter.

The development of the mediation institute in Poland occurred on two parallel tracks. On the one hand, mediations over the years outsourced companies have acquired increasingly important, centers have been set up of mediation at Chambers of Commerce or with other business organizations. On the other hand, the attempt by them tribunals to use mediation for causes in matters of family law and civil law. Current Art. 183, paragraph 2, §3 of the Code of Civil Procedure Civil Procedure, indicates the requirements that must be in the mediator's possession. Civil disputes can play the role of mediator any physical person not forbidden and which also possesses the skills and ability of conduct mediation proceedings, which I have 26 years old, have knowledge of the language Polish, did not have final convictions for deliberate crimes and has not been subjected to any proceedings for such offenses. The District Court, after verifying the veracity of the data reported in the registration form, proceeds with the inscription of the subject's name applicant in the lists of professional mediators. At present, it is up to the parties to appoint the mediator and, only when the parties do not provide such a choice or in case of contrast or, in any case, in cases of failure appoint the Tribunal, in dismissing the parties to mediation, also means a mediator who has the appropriate skills.

The inclusion of the costs of the mediation, carried out following referral by the Court, in the so-called costs of judgment. Another relevant amendment concerns the possibility of get the full refund of the so-called judgment tax, in cases where the parties reach an agreement already during the phase preliminary, or conclude the agreement, both in court and through a mediator before assessing the merits of controversy, or before the hearing. The full refund of that quota is anyway following the conclusion of the agreement.

The approved agreement has the same legal value as one any judgment issued by a judge.

In Estonia: Mediation can be done by the Chancellor of Justice who controls whether the bodies public respect the rights and fundamental freedoms of the citizens and the principles of good conduct administrative.

The conciliation procedure before the Registrar is governed by Article 35, points 5 to 15 of the law on the Chancellor of Justice. Mediation is voluntary, but participation in the cases established by law are a condition of procedural. It can be preventive or delegated by the judge. It can be exercised directly by natural persons and therefore does not require accreditation at a Body. The mediator is formed by the Association of the mediators and becomes such as a result of oath.

The Estonian Civil Procedure Code contains one special rule that provides for conciliation at work of the judge in situations where a parent violates one a measure concerning the right of the child to visit.

In Latvia: There is no state-level body at all entral to the regulation of the mediator profession.

There are several private organizations that you they engage in mediation.

There is an institute called izlīgums. This is an agreement with which parties are doing reciprocal concessions.

Izlīgums is allowed at any stage of the procedure and any civil controversy, ad Except for the cases provided by the Rite Code. The judge may approve the izlīgums in the absence of the parties, if it has been certified by a notary and contains one declaration of the parties attesting to their awareness about the procedural consequences that derive from the approval of the agreement.

However, prior to the approval of the Court of First Instance check whether the parties have agreed the izlīgums voluntarily and in accordance with the provisions of the Rite code.

If successful, it agrees the agreement. Mediation is admissible in the civil sector, in family law and criminal law. Mediation is not free and the amount depends by the mediator 's experience and the difficulty of the dispute. The mediation agreement is enforced in force of Community Directive n. 2008/52 / EC[23].

In Lithuania: In 2008, it became a law on mediation. Mediation originates or from an agreement that can intervene during a dispute or antecedently or it may be the judge ad send the parties in mediation. Judicial mediation is held within the local court, and the procedure does not last longer than four hours, although the mediator may require one time supplement at the occurrence. Agreements have the force of law; If This is an out-of-court mediation agreement be homologated by simplified procedure by DistricMediators are formed at private entities. The mediators' fees are agreed between the parties.

The agreement may be enforceable by the parties which they signed it by referring to the Directive of European Community, no. 2008/52 / EC[24].

---

[23] https://mediaresenzaconfini.org/category/lettonia/t court of residence of the parties.
[24] https://mediaresenzaconfini.org/2012/02/27/la mediazione-in-pillolelettonia/

In Luxembourg: the use of mediation is optional and is admissible for disputes penalties, family law, commercial and litigation neighborhood. The procedure lasts three months and can be started by the parties, by the judge or by virtue of a clause contractual. There is no national deontological code for mediators, or a central body for the regulators of mediators. The University of Luxembourg offers a specific training program (university degree) in mediation. Mediation is not free, but the services of mediation are subject to a fee agreed between the private broker and the parties of the dispute.

The mediation agreement is not signed by the mediator, unless the parties do not require it. Directive No. 2008/52 / EC allows the parties to ask for the content of a written agreement resulting from a mediation being rendered enforceable. According to the case law of the Court of Justice relating to the Brussels Convention of 1968 judicial transactions and mediation agreements, constitute "decisions" within the meaning of Article 25 of the Convention, as such acts cover essentially contractual character. In the event of a conflict between a judgment rendered litigation and an agreement, the latter it can assimilate to a judicial transaction, not allows you to oppose the exequatur request judgment.

State subsidies for non-residents it also applies to mediation. Judicial assistance is in fact granted in this matter extrajudicial and judicial, non-litigious or litigation, to all parties in dispute.

Slovenia: from 2001-2009 the Courts have used the mediation to reach a provisional agreement subsequently refined by the judge. The experience of the programs was resumed in one new law of 2009. Courts may order mediation obligatory information and who does not pay expenses.

The new law on mediation in 2008 has instead transposed the UNCITRAL regolations on conciliation.

Mediation is free in terms of relationships between parents and children and on dismissal. In civil matters, mediation is free for the first three hours, while in commercial matters, they are litigants have to pay in equal shares to make mediation.

Every organism that wants to exercise must get authorization. In particular, he must have a list of mediators, to demonstrate mediation for at least three years, to own premises and equipment according to regulation, to comply with current hygiene rules, building standards, those for protection environmental, urban planning, legislation in safety and fire protection. Each mediator must play at least ten mediations per year to stay in the list[25].

Slovakia: Mediation is governed by one 2004 law updated in 2010 for implementation of Directive 52/08. Mediation covers all matters of law. Start with a contract that must be registered in notary register. The agreement can be transposed in a ruling or by a deed. The discipline of the organisms, the bodies of training and training requirements to be mediators is similar to the Italian one (the course is however 100 hours). An exam is also supported for updating.

---

[25]https://mediaresenzaconfini.org/2012/01/16/la mediazione-in-pilloleslovenia

The mediator can not oppose professional secrecy if the judgment concerns its liability. The fee for the mediator is hourly[26].

In Croatia: Mediation is chargeable, yes volunteer, except in terms of work when it comes to it strike, or even divorce with children minors or finally when a Croatian citizen wants to sue against the state and vice versa. Under the Mediation Act, published in the Official Gazette of Republic of Croatia, hereinafter referred to as "NN") no. 18/11, e of mediator register rules and requirements for the accreditation of the mediation bodies and of the mediators (NN 59/11), the Ministry of Justice he has the task of keeping the register of mediators.

The mediation bodies are:

- Mediation Center at the Chamber of the Croatian Economy (2002).

- Permanent Court of Arbitration at the Chamber of the Croatian Economy.

---

[26]https://mediaresenzaconfini.org/2012/01/12/la mediazione-inpilloleslovacchia/

- Mediation Center at the Association of Croatian employers (2004).

- Mediation Center at the Association lawyers in Croatia (2004).

- Office for Social Partnership (controversies collective work; 2003).

- Social Assistance Centers (mediate and are partners for the implementation of the right to family).

- Professional services dealing with agreements extrajudicial (criminal mediation, 2001).

- Center for Peace.

In Sweden: mediation is possible both civil and criminal. There are no national bodies established for training of mediators. The mediator does not have a code of ethics respect and the use of ADR is left to the will of the parties as well as the determination of the remuneration to the mediator.

The mediation agreement is enforced in force of Community Directive n. 2008/52 / EC.

In Norway: the law was issued in 1991 introduction to mediation in civil matters criminal.

The procedure is free and is organized on three levels: 1) Local Conflict Council; 2) Secretariat local councils; 3) Ministry of Justice. The Secretariat is the reference body from the point of technical view and training under supervision of the Ministry of Justice.

The mediator must meet certain requirements:

- Must enjoy electoral rights.

- should not have been condemned too suspensively for crimes in the previous five years at the first mediation.

- You must not have been condemned or end up under trial in the ten years prior to the nomination.

In each municipality of the territory is prepared a mediation board that has two representatives appointed by the City Council for four years from the municipal police.

In case one of the parties participating in the mediation is the Public Administration mediation is governed by administrative law.

The Courts make a big application of an old man law mediation law of 2005[27], which states iter procedural to be followed in case of conflict.

Indeed, the parties before a trial will check whether it is possible a friendly composition before conciliation board. The procedure lasts three months, and is renewable. Conciliation is introduced with a complaint to the conciliation board to be notified to the defendant which has two weeks to answer. At the conciliation meeting the parties may be also assisted by a qualified attorney for assist the parties in front of the Conciliation Board. Conciliation attempt is mandatory that:

---

[27] Dispute Act 2005/90
(http://www.ub.uio.no/ujur/ulovdata/lov- 2005/90
(http://www.ub.uio.no/ujur/ulovdata/lov-20050617-090-eng.pdf).

(a) the value of the dispute exceeds 125,000 NOK and both parties are assisted by a lawyer.

b) a mediation attempt has already been made out-of-court.

c) the case has been heard by another court.

The scope is general and can also cover small ones claims, but there are some excluded subjects such as family matter, unless the issue matters exclusively the Financial Regulation of the separation, in the disputes they see as a public authority, institution or a public authority official on issues that are not exclusive in private law, in cases concerning the validity of a arbitration award or an out-of-court composition, in cases where the law provides that the decisions of the court are binding on the parties, or even in those in which the law excludes the attempt to conciliation. The Conciliation Board can make proposals and express points of view on the story or issue judgment.

The parties may also resort to out of court mediation agreed by contract, choosing together with the mediator from the panel of the Court. Unlike prior conciliation in front of Conciliation board, this mediation is not free. Mediation can also be initiated by the judge during the process. The judge may also be the mediator of the case and if so in the same conciliation fails it can always Express an opinion. The areas of application of mediation are the family law, commercial and labor law. There is no obligation to train mediators.

The agreement must result from the minutes[28].

In Bulgaria: there is no mediation agency public but private associations.

Since 2010, the Center has also been established dispute settlement, consisting of: brokers working in turn, providing daily free mediation services and information to parties in pending processes. The Minister of Justice has introduced in the register of legal entities a register of mediators. Mediation is not free and the remuneration to the mediator is not related to the result.

---

[28]https://mediaresenzaconfini.files.wordpress.com/2012/02/sistemi-dicomposizione- conflict-of-in-Cyprus-Norway-and-in-malta.pdf

Within this log, in addition to the list mediators qualified to exercise the profession, the private organizations represented at the training and updating mediators within the territory.

There is no code of conduct for mediators, is a voluntary procedure applied in the field civil, commercial and corporate and is not subject to gratuity. The agreement reached at mediation can be rendered enforceable by making express request to competent authorities, as provided for in the note European Directive 2008/52 / EC[29].

In Denmark: mediation is not disciplined by law.

The law provides for the use of mediation in the civil cases before a district court, regional, maritime and trade, as well as in the criminal cases. Chapter 27 of the Law on Administration of justice (retsplejeloven) defines, in fact, the rules on court mediation in cases civilians in the district courts (District Courts), the Østre Landsret (Regional Court of Denmark) or the Vestre Landsret (regional court)

---

[29] https://www.ar-net.it/category/mediazione-in-europa/

of western Denmark) and the So-og Handelsretten (maritime court and trade).

If the civil judge considers mediation to be appropriate the case may appoint a judicial mediator for a civil mediation (Retsmægling). The mediator may be a judge or an official of the competent court or a lawyer who has been considered appropriate.

The formation of the mediator is attributed to the Domstolstyrelsen (administration of organs Danish judiciary) to act as mediator in the district of a regional jurisdiction court.

The cost of the mediation is timetable and the indemnity of mediation, when the mediator is a judge, they go added travel expenses[30].

In the Netherlands: Mediation is applied in the field civil, it is optional, it is not free and it is not compulsory legal assistance. There is the institute of Mediation naast rechtspraak ("Mediation alongside justice"). The District Court or the Court of Appeal

---

[30] www.fiscooggi.it/dal.../mediation-ue-danimarca-tempo-regola-costodella- Mediation

at which may be litigated may indicate to the interested in the choice of mediation when the dispute so requires. An independent center is Nederlands Mediation Instituut (NMI, Center for Mediation of Countries Bass) holding the list of mediators that are formed with private organizations. The agreement signed by the parties is enforceable in force of Community Directive n. 2008/52 / EC.

In Spain: Ley 5/2012 of 6 July, received the European directive and regulated mediation civil and commercial. It finds application in collective work that individual and family is handled in shape voluntary.

The organ overseen by the mediation promoted in the various courts is Consejo General of the Poder Judici (General Council of the Judiciary) that it can also rely on the aid of the Communities Autonomous (the Spanish Regions), Universities, of Municipalities and Associations for its dissemination. As regards the training obligations of the mediators, the law states that he / she must own one university degree, and a specification mediation training that can be acquired through the attendance of courses prematurely practical with a duration of between 100 and the 300 hours offered by the University and Orders Professional. The agreement reached in mediation acquires effectiveness executed if provided by the notary's intervention. It should be remembered that the Treaty on Union European (Maastricht, 1992) based in Strasbourg has established a body with the function of guaranteeing impartiality and the good performance of the public European administration, reporting on its own initiative if necessary, abuses, shortcomings and delays to citizens of European Union.

This is the European Ombudsman who knows of the art. 228 T.F.U.E (Operation Treaty of the European Union) is elected by Parliament for the term of the legislature with a mandate renewable. It is a European Institutional charge that is able to receive complaints of any citizen of the Union or of any natural or legal person residing or having the place of business in a Member State, concerning cases of maladministration in the action of institutions, organs and bodies of the Union European with the exception of the Court of Justice and of the Court of First Instance in the exercise of judicial function.

They do not, however, fall within the competences of European Ombudsman cases concerning the national, regional or local administrations, though the allegations relate to alleged violations of the Community law.

The European Ombudsman acts in full independence from any power, including from European Parliament.

As soon as he receives the complaint, the Ombudsman proceeds to the appropriate investigations and informs the institution or the organ concerned.

The complaint must be filed within two years from the date on which the facts justify it are brought to the attention of the concerned citizen.

It does not interrupt the terms for appeals in judicial or administrative proceedings and must be preceded by the appropriate administrative steps at the competent institutions or bodies.

State authorities are obliged to provide the mediator at your request through the representations permanent Member States of the Union European

Union, all the information that can contributeto shed light on cases of maladministration by the side of the institutions or bodies of the Union, except where:

such information is subject to provisions laws or regulations on secrecy professional or otherwise prohibiting it

publication. In such a last resort, the Member State could allow access provided that it does not come disclosed the content (Article 3, paragraph 3, dec. 94/262 / ECSC, EC, Euratom). Unlike if not he receives the information the Ombudsman makes known of that conducted by the European Parliament, which takes over initiatives of the case (Article 3 (4) of Decree 94/262 / ECSC, EC, Euratom). An action may be brought against the Ombudsman's acts for damages based on liability non-contractual union. The European Ombudsman can not be removed from Parliament's assignment: always second Article. 228, par. The second paragraph of Article 2 of the Treaty Operation of the European Union, Parliament may only bring an action before the Court of Justice justice with which he asks to resign mediator, but it is up to the Court to decide.

CHAPTER IV

THE REFORM OF CIVIL MEDIA AND COMMERCIAL

Civil and commercial mediation is a new one civil dispute resolution system alternative to ordinary judgment before the Court of First Instance or the Judge of Peace, conducted by an impartial third party (mediator), assisting two or more subjects, in seeking a friendly agreement.

The State regulated this sector through:

- Legislative Decree no. 28 of 4 March 2010;

- Ministerial Decree no. 180 of 18 October 2010;

- Decree of 6 July 2011 n. 145 - Rules of Procedure modification to d.m 18 October 2010, no. 180, on determination of the criteria and methods of registration and keeping the register of mediation bodies and of the list of mediators, as well as on the approval of benefits payable to organisms, pursuant to art. 16 of the d. lgs. 28/2010;

- Law Decree June 21, 2013 n. 69 conv. In Law 9 August 2013 n. 98;

- The Ministerial Circular on November 27, 2013;

- Decree 4 August 2014 n. 139 - Regulation laying down Amendment to the Justice Decree of 18 October 2010 n. 180

The decree-law of June 21, 2013, no. 69 (decree "of the do, "converted into law August 9, 2013 n. 98) ha restoring the mediation process as the legality of the proceedings in the subjects listed in Article 5, paragraph 1 of the Legislative Decree 28/2010, and, introduced new standards.

In detail:

• It is expected to be compulsory on the subject of real rights, division and hereditary succession, family pacts, lease and rent, rent of companies, compensation for damages from liability medical and health, defamation with the medium printing or advertising, contracts insurance, banking and financial contracts, condominium, and in case of dismissal from the work.

• A criterion of competence has been included territory for the submission of the application.

- A meeting of programming before the meeting of mediation, it is a condition of procedure, to be completed within 30 days from instance deposit, free in case of failure to adhere to mediation.

- Rc car disputes are excluded from the materials as they are added disputes concerning damages resulting from responsibility (not just medical but more widely) sanitary.

- Tax incentives are introduced such as the exemption from stamp duty or from any tax or right of any kind and nature for all acts, documents and measures if with mediation resolves the conflict;

from the tax record of the Agreed Minute for the value of 50,000 euros and a credit of sets to the corresponding parts the expected bonus up to 500 EUR.

- Also mediation procedures can be managed only by public bodies and private iscritti to a special register near of the ministry of justice and that mediators, enrolled in the list of bodies accredited to register, have attended and passed a special training course delivered by accredited by the Ministry of Education giustizia[31].

• Mediation can be activated either by will of the parties or under a clause contractual or by delegation of the judge during the course of an ordinary judgment.

• The judge can also order, and not only invite, parties to proceed to mediation before the hearing of clarification of the conclusions or before the discussion of the case. When mediation is condition of the applicability of the application court, the court convicts the party constituted, which does not participate in the proceedings without justification, to the payment of one sum equal to the unified contribution. From also remember the judgment of the Court of Appeal of Milan, of 10 May 2017 in the cause r.g. n. 4004/2016 where it was sanctioned with the penalty of the impracticability of the application the conduct of the parties they did not want continue mediation by the judge after the first meeting.

---

[31] www.ar-net.it

- the Court of Appeal of Milan, with the judgment of 28 June 2017 intervened to put clarity over the 15 day deadline set by judge, claiming it does not correspond to one procedural time to apply the disposition of which in art. 154 c.p.c. . It follows that defectof an explicit sanction, the condition of procedurality is also to be considered occurred when the first was done meeting before the mediator, following the late deposit of the application for mediation.

However delay (eg 4 months after expiry of the term given by the judge) does not have to be such as to affect the performance of the process, to the detriment of the application (Court of Vasto judgment of 27 September 2017).

- The entire procedure ends within 3 months from the filing date of the application.

Recently, the judgment of the Rome, section VIII civil, of October 22, 2014 has established that "this time limit can not that it only works for usability of applications at court and not, vice versa, constitute a time limit for the formation of the agreement ".

It follows that the agreements are valid achieved beyond the expiration date.

• New in favor of lawyers is the circular of the Ministry of Justice of 2 December 2013 n. prot. 168322 which, after its entry into force of the art. 84 of the "decree of making" in the field of civil and commercial mediation, has introduced new directives such as:

(a) Obligatory presence of the lawyer including "compulsory mediations" the one prepared by the judge pursuant to art. 5 paragraph 2, with the exception of materials optional parts left to the parties faculty to avail of the assistance of the legal.

b) to the lawyer mediator, with the limit imposed by art. 55-bis, paragraph 4 of the forensic deontological code: "it is done prohibition to the lawyer to allow that the body shall have its seat, in any way, at his or her studio seat at the mediation body ".

• The Circular of 14 July 2015 establishes, instead, cases of incompatibilities and conflicts of interest of mediators attorneys:

(a) The Confederation of mediation at Forensi Orders and all attorneys enrolled in the Order are incompatible forense itself when exercising, like mediator or defender, before the bodies of mediation of the Forensic Order to which belong, since the principle of third party and impartiality that must characterize the Body and the Mediators - lawyers registered in the mediation process.

(b) The Organization is in conflict of interest use facilities, staff and staff mediators of other bodies with whom I have reached an agreement for this purpose, even for individuals mediation business, ex art.7, comma 2, lett. c) D. M. 180/2010. Attorneys have the obligation to professional upgrade.

• There has been a new discipline on the subject of mediation procedure in detail:

The procedure begins with the deposit in secretary of the mediation application signed by the instant part and the lawyer, together with the ID card copy and copy of the payment of the start-up costs of euro 48,80 by wire transfer bank / post office.

The secretary sends the request to the Responsible of the Organism, who assigns the mediation business to accredited mediators.

The Manager, after checking the regularity of the documentation forms a file by assigning a protocol number of which a copy is sent to the mediator after that he has accepted the appointment in writing signed the declaration of impartiality[32].

The Responsible establishes the programmatic meeting not later than 30 days from the filing of the application;

The parties may ask the ADR Secretariat Request for Referral not more than 8 days prior to date of the first meeting. Later, the secretary performs the communications to the agreed party by means of pec or registered with return receipt in which he becomes aware that he will participate in one informative meeting in a day and now fixed from the Organism. The meeting of programming can end:

---

[32] www.giustizia.it/giustizia/en/mg_2_7_11.wp

- Negatively, one of the parts is absent. According to the order issued by the Verona, 11 May 2017, no. 1626 the part which confers special proxy on something else subject, including his defender, can do it represent in the mediation process without fear of falling into improvisability.

In that case, the Ombudsman forms a verbal negative of non-participation at the meeting, signed by the present, releasing a copy to the applicant and copying it in secretary, with the closing of the procedure. In this case no compensation is due to the Organism.

- Positively, with the participation of all the parties (instant, defendant, lawyers and the mediator appointed by the Body). In sitting the Ombudsman will ask the participants if they intend to continue the next meeting to resolve the dispute by mediating inviting them he was before that meeting to perform the payment of the allowance provided by the Ministry of Justice and Living Expenses giving a reasonable time to execute them, specifying that the requested party must to make in addition to the allowance also the start-up costs and living expenses not yet filed. They must be paid not less than half.

Failure to comply with this obligation entails closure of the same for non-payment half of the costs of mediation.

The secretary shall carry out the appropriate checks and only later the parties, the lawyers and the Ombudsman will discuss the cause at the conclusion of which (positive or negative) the parts will pay the residual allowance that will entitle them the release of the minutes.

At the 1st mediation meeting, the conciliator hear the parties and their lawyers and try on conciliation. If the conciliation is successful positive is a verbal, signed by all those who participated in the mediation, to which the text is attached Agreement.

In the mandatory subjects the assistance of the attorneys attesting and certifying the compliance of the agreement with the mandatory rules and public order is a title executive for forced expropriation, for execution for delivery and release, the fulfillment of obligations to do and not to do, as well as for the registration of a legal mortgage. According to art. 12 of the decree of making the agreement referred to in the preceding period must to be fully transcribed in the precept to pursuant to art. 480, second paragraph of the code of civil procedure. In all other cases the agreement annexed to the minutes, at the request of part, is homologated by the Court, and constitutes enforceable title for forced expropriation, for execution in a specific form, as well as for the registration of a legal mortgage. From the outcome of the meeting or lack, the mediator gives it act in the minutes and put it in mail.

Before delivering the parts provide for the balance of the expenditure due subsequently released their copy of the simple request.

In accordance with D.lgs. 28/2010 art. 1, comma 1 lett. (a) is delivered at the end of also process an evaluation board of the service, signed by the parties to be telematic transmission to the Manager.

When the meeting took place at a venue detached, their responsible people are committed to send a copy of the above documents to the secretary at half-pec.

All the burdens, including the tax revenues by the agreement reached, shall be borne by the set off.

At any time of the proceedings, the mediator can make a proposal of conciliation or agreement of the set off.

Communication of the request of completing the conciliation attempt interrupts the prescription and suspends, for the its duration the course of each term of decadence.

It was inserted in art. 2643 c.c. paragraph 12 bis according to which they are subject to transcription " the mediation agreements that ensure the usucation with the subscription of the process verbal authenticated by a public official a this is authorized. " It follows that the mediation record, constitutes a title of determination, devoid of translational effects, which once authenticated by a notary, is a suitable title for transcribing the transfer of the property and to ascertain the purchase of the property at the head of the part that has activated mediation.

From March 1, 2015, the Ministry of Justice it envisaged in the circular of 18 September 2014 the Registration of Organizations of mediation and training bodies on the computer system, term extended to 6 April 2015.

From that date, therefore, on the website of the site of the Ministry of Justice, under the heading Mediation and Listing Agency Register Training bodies, are the only ones Organizations that have forwarded to administer all data via the computer system.

The administration, after validating the data inserted by the bodies and bodies which, in the their own interest, have provided the the requirements set out in points 2 and 3 of the above circular, provide for insertion in the new log and in the new list and to obscure the data on the old register and on the old one list.

The latter, are destined to to disappear. Lastly, it is noted that only the organisms and the Entities that register on the computer system see inserted I mediators and trainers' names, in the appropriate list of brokers and brokers trainers referred to in art. 3, paragraphs 3 and 17, paragraph 3, D.M. 180/2010.

By order, the State Council of 22 April 2015 n. 1694, partially suspended the enforceability of the TAR Lazio judgment no. 1351/2015, stated that they are due, for the first mediation meeting, startup costs and the documented living expenses incurred by the Organization for managing the procedure.

Mediation allowance is not due when the parties that participated in the session preliminary information decides not to continue. Mediation allowance includes:

- the costs of initiating the proceedings (summons, email or email alerts) of € 40.00 VAT for controversies of value not exceeding € 250,000 and € 80,00 VAT for controversies of value higher.

- the costs of mediation indicated in Table A reported on the ministerial decree are due in solid from each party that adhered to method.

If they are more than one subject they represent one centers of interest are considered as a single part.

- are added to the indemnity, the living expenses (costs per videoconference services, and other documented expenses and due to the procedure) and the payment of a fund for each communication by letter A / R recommended or via notification Bailiff.

According to art. 16, paragraph 4 of the D.M. 180/2010 e sue ss. Mm. And ii. are also due to the eventuality bonuses calculated on the basis of the basic rates from the Table A attached to the Decree, in particular:

- an increase of ¼ for the agreement reached.

- 1/5 increase for the conciliation proposal formulated by the mediator at the request of the parties (only in the case of voluntary mediation and arising from contractual clause).

- 1/5 extra for special disputes importance, complexity and difficulty.

- in the matters referred to in art. 5, paragraph 1, of Legislative Decree no. 28/2010 must be reduced by 1/3 for the first 6 shifts and half for the rest, save the reduction for the case of non-appearance of counterparties.

The bonuses do not apply except that of ¼ if mediation succeeds (Letter B, 16).

- must be reduced to € 40.00 for the first installment and € 50.00 for the remaining ones when none of them counterparts of the one that introduced the mediation, participate in the proceedings. The allowance remains fixed even if it changes mediator during the proceeding or comes appointed a college of mediators. The sums owed are paid to the Organization or by bank transfer or by newsletter post.

The value of the claim is indicated in the application of mediation and if the value is indeterminate the mediation body that has taken over question will decide the reference value up to limit of € 250,000. They have been provided by art. 8 paragraph 5 of Legislative Decree no. 28/2010 as amended by L.98 / 2013, sanctions against parties that do not participate in mediation without any justified reason (legitimate impediment, because of force majeure, the missed or late communication of the site of day or hour of meeting, error in person, the nullity of mediation, incompetence territorial organization of the Organization, the defect of legitimacy of the party).

In fact, it reads that "from the lack of participation the judge can infer test arguments in subsequent judgment under art. 116, 2nd paragraph of the civil procedure code.

The judge convicts the constituted party, in cases provided for in Article 5, did not take part in the proceedings without justification, to the payment at the entry of the state budget of an amount of money corresponding to the unified contribution due for the judgment. " The value you expect to benefit from free sponsorship year 2017 is 11,528.41 euros.

It is envisaged that telematic mediation can be implemented if the parties both agree with one party participate in videoconferencing and the other, participate physically in the presence of the mediator in the seat Body.

At the end of the meeting, the parties may receive directly in electronic format through Certified Electronic Mail Certified Circuit (ed eventually later on domicile) a copy of the minutes certifying the terms and the terms of the agreement reached, that is, the declaration of non-agreement;

The signing of the minutes can take place either with telematic mode (digital signature), both in mode analogue (autographed signature).

If digital signature is not available, the minutes and agreements must be signed during the meeting in videoconferencing and telematic messaging from Ombudsman to the Parties, who provide the press for the purpose of subscribing and authenticating signatures to an official public.

The Parties then send the paperwork documentation to Ombudsman verifying the correspondence of the minutes and authenticated agreements with those signed in videoconferencing.

In accordance with the third paragraph of art. 11, D.lgs 4/3/2010 n. 28, in the event that the parties make one of the acts of which in art. 2643 c.c., the signing of the verb goes "Authenticated by an official public to this authorized. " On June 23, 2017, it was published in the Gazette Official conversion of the CD. manovrina. This is the Decree-Law of 24 April 2017, n. 50, converted, with modifications, into the law 21 June 2017, no. 96, on urgent provisions in financial matters, initiatives in favor of the entities territorial, further interventions for affected areas seismic events and development measures. Among the various interventions there is one provision in mediation: Art. 11-ter. Article. 11-ter modifies art. 5, paragraph 1-bis, d.lgs. 4 March 2010, no. 28 who, as is well known, said discipline of the c.d. compulsory mediation ante causam or ex lege: hypothesis in which, parts of one civil or commercial litigation are obligatory, before turning to the judge, to experiment (by the penalty of impracticability of the application) mediation; this is the case for disputes in the subjects listed in art. 5, paragraph 1-bis, d.lgs. 28/2010. The main novelty introduced in this regard art. 11-ter, d.l. 50/2017, convention, with mod., In the. 96/2017, consists in stabilizing in the ordinance the effectiveness of the discipline of the mandatory mediation which, before the c.d. maneuver 2017, had transient nature and experimental. The temporary character is then deleted dell'istituto[33]. Recently, the Court of Naples, sect. VI ordinance 05/02/2019 reiterated the recourse to a second attempt at mediation in the same proceedings, when the first sentence had ended with a negative outcome.

---

[33] www.altalex.com/documents/news/2017/07/06/medical-manualsupport.

CHAPTER V

MEDIATION CHARACTERISTICS

IMPARTIALITY'

The mediator is an impartial third.

SPEED '

The procedure of mediation lasts 3 months.

CONFIDENTIALITY

What emerges during meetings can not to be detected by the mediators, this obligation is enshrined in the confidentiality agreement signed by mediator to the act of the acceptance of the job and protected at trial.

ECONOMY '

Mediation costs are lower than one Ordinary judgment that lasts several years.

The conciliation record is exempt from tax register up to the amount of 50,000 euros and the tax is due only to the excess part. In the event of a successful mediation, the parties have entitled to a tax credit up to a maximum of ninety two 500 euros that can indicate in the incomes.

In the event of a failure of the mediation, the credit tax is reduced by half.

f) AUTONOMY

The agreement has the value of a contract and its execution is left to the will of the parties.

INTERRUPTION OF PRESCRIPTION

The activation of the mediation process interrupts the prescription and suspends, for the duration the conciliation attempt and the twenty days following its conclusion, the course of each term of decadence.

CHAPTER VI

MEDIA DEMAND

The application for mediation must contain the requirements as indicated in art. 4 of Legislative Decree 28/2010, in particular:

Instant part: name and surname, residence, address, tax code, VAT ID, cell and / or tel, fax, email, name of legal representative with indication of law firm, address and cell or tel, tax code, fax, email, pec.

Invited party: name and surname, residence, address, tax code, VAT ID, cell and / or tel, fax, email, name of legal representative with indication of law firm, address and cell or tel, tax code, fax, email, pec.

Subject of the application with a brief description of the dispute Indicator of the mediator, indication of the place preferred mediation (optional).

The Mediation Body

The value of the dispute

Attachments

The application for mediation must match always to the content of the claim otherwise it would be a new question that the judge would declare improper. In the case of a necessary litis consortium, these must be called in the mediation phase, otherwise at the procedural stage the question could be eclared improvised to him, except that the Organization does not foresee an integration successiva[34].

---

[34] BOGGIO, Mediation and Defense, Milan, 2011, 28.

The application for mediation is as compulsory in the cases mentioned in 1 paragraph of art. 5 of Legislative Decree no. 28/2010, while I am except those covered by the fourth paragraph. Recently, the Court of Rovigo with a judgment of the 17.3.2017 has stated that "in opposition to a injunction, the burden of trying the attempt Mandatory mediation concerns the part contrary to what provided for by art. 5 of d.lgs. n. 28 of 2010 "at the expense of improvisability.

CHAPTER VII

THE ROLE OF THE LAWYER, THE PARTIES, IL OMBUDSMAN

1. THE ROLE OF THE ADVOCATE

The mediator's role has always been subject to regulatory changes not only national but also European. The underlying ratio was that of to ensure the right to a qualified defense to the citizen, even in mediation procedures[35].

The agreement reached on 12/05/2011 between the Ministry of Justice and the Law Firm in which it was made the presence of the lawyer in mediation is compulsory it had this purpose.

In fact, the Ministerial Circular of 2 December 2013 n. prot. 168322 states, on the one hand, that presence of the mediator's lawyer was mandatory in subjects of cui to the art. 5, paragraph 1 and those indicated

---

[35] President of the National Board of Trustees Guido Alpa in the Journal of Sicily of 12/05/2011 p. 9.

in the art. 5, paragraph 2. For voluntary mediation parties could participate without being assisted of the lawyer, with the faculty to avail any phase of the procedure.

From the other to the senses of the art. 16 of Legislative Decree no. 28/2010 that: "Attorneys enrolled in mediation bodies they had to be adequately trained in mediation and keep up with your preparation theoretical-practical update paths to this finalizzati, in the respect of what foreseen of the art. 55 bis of the forensic code of conduct ". The organization of these courses was left to the Council National forensics and district orders to the senses of the art. 11 Law 31 December 2012 n. 247. According to art. 55-bis, paragraph 4 of the Code deontological is prohibited by the lawyer of allow the mediation body to have it home, in any way, at his or her studio viceversa[36].

Subsequently, in the Ministerial Circular of 14 July 2015, the case of incompatibility was regulated of the lawyer with that of the mediator. In particular,

---

[36] www.mediazioneindipendente.it

the lawyer / mediator was denied the possibility to intervene in the same case as legal and as mediator at the same time later.

A provision which was annulled by the new judgment of the Tar Lazio, sect. I, judgment of 9 March - 1 April 2016, no. 3989.

There was a violation of art. 3 and 41 Cost, what a breach of the principles of equality of treatment, freedom of economic initiative and of competition.

Breach of Art. 4 of Directive 2008/52 / EC of the European Parliament and of the Council European Parliament and Council of 21 May 2008. Excess of power for unreasonableness and disparity of treatment.

Violation of the right of defense referred to in art. 24 Cost as it prevented the subject he wanted protect your own right to turn to your own trusted professional for the sole fact that this he is a member of the mediation body to mediate between the parties or even to be simply associate or associate or "roommate" of a professional member of the specific body of mediation.

It is recalled that, pursuant to art. 4, 3rd paragraph of Legislative Decree no. n. 28/2010 the lawyer has duties towards the Customer in particular must:

- Inform the client in writing of the obligation to use the mediation procedure provided by the d.lgs. n. 28/2010, for rights disputes available on:

condominium, real rights, division, successions heritages, family patties, lease, commodity, renting of companies, compensation of the resulting damages from vehicle and boat traffic, compensation damages from medical liability, damages from defamation with the press or other means means of advertising, insurance contracts, banking and Financial.

- Inform the tax incentives provided by the Articles. 17 and 20 of Legislative Decree no. n. 28/2010.

- from 29 August 2017, has the obligation to submit to the own customer a cost estimate for Out-of-court assistance, concerning the procedure of mediation.

Additionally,

- has the duty to check if the agreement has the validity and effectiveness requirements of the law.

- can not replace the customer. In fact, the party has to present yourself personally in the meetings and if it is impossible can not be replaced by his lawyer, it may instead ask for the presence of another subject with substantive delegation ad hoc (Tribunal of Pavia, sez. III civil, ordinance 14.09.2015)[37].

The document signed by the assistant must be annexed to the introductory document of a judgment, (citation or appeal act) at the time of the entry in the case of the case brought in even from authorization to data processing personal, as foreseen by the art.13 of the D.Lgs. 196/2003.

Violation of the standard involves an illicit disciplinary for the lawyer.

"The ignorance of the information, far different from the lover in the exercise of the customer's duty of care, it affects the more general duty to be correct behavior "(C.N.F., 14.4.1993, No 68).

The mediation agreement signed by the parties and by attorneys is enforceable for forced expropriation, execution for delivery and performance of

---

[37] www.altalex.com

obligations to do or not, as well as for the registration of a legal mortgage (Article 12, paragraph 1);

Among the novelties, there are changes at the level community, in which the non-emergence emerges necessary presence of the lawyer in mediation.

In the 2013 / EU Directive, the hypothesis is excluded of the obligatory assistance of a lawyer in the a course of mediation aimed at solving a dispute between professionals and consumers, leaving the parties free about handling the procedure.

Next, the European Court of Justice, Sect. I, with the ruling of 14/06/2017, No. C-75/16, according to which: "one national legislation can not impose on the consumer who takes part in an Adr procedure to be assisted by such a lawyer taken is contrary to Community law ".

2. THE PARTS

The parties are active subjects of mediation, which determine whether or not they succeed.

They can be both natural and public or private, single or multiple parts together.

In the light of the last judgments their participation personal (assisted by your defenders, such as provided for in art. 8, I co. of D.Lgs. 28/2010, as amended by D.L. June 22, 2013, No.69, converted with modifications by L. 9 August 2013, n. 98) is required both for mediation compulsory to be conducted before the judgment ex art. 5, paragraph 1 bis, D. Lgs. 28/2010, both for the mediation demanded by the judge, ex art. 5, paragraph 2, for the purpose of respecting the procedural requirement of the application (Ordinance of 2-05-2016, the Court of First Instance, Vasto, ruling 09/03/2015, Tribunal of Pordenone, judgment 10.3.2017).

In fact, failure to participate is subject to sanction ex art. 8, paragraph 4-bis and the ex-sanction art. 96 c.p.c. In particular, delegated mediation the Tribunal of Reggio has intervened Emilia, by order of 26.04.2017 affirming that: "the mediation attempt is indeed started and that the parties - rather than limit themselves to meet and inquire, not adhering to Ombudsman's proposal to proceed – fulfill actually in the court order by participating to the real mediation procedure, save the existence of questions referred for a preliminary ruling prevent procedurality ". Recently, revised by the ordinance issued by Court of Verona of 11 May 2017, no. 1626.

3. THE MEDIATOR

The mediator is an expert in conciliation techniques, which strives for the parties to reach a friendly agreement (Art.8, paragraph 3, Legislative Decree 28/2010). The requirements for becoming a mediator are:

- possession of a degree of study not lower than the degree three years or alternatively that they are subscribed to an order or to a professional college (surveyors, surveyors industrialists, agricultural experts, labor consultants, architects, engineers, accountants).

- possessing a trained training following a 50 hours training course that includes courses practical theorists and a final test of 4 hours, at an accredited mediation body.

- Honor

- Conduct of 20 cases of mediation at the Mediation Bodies or Chambers of Commerce accredited.

- Perform a two - yearly update of 18 hours.

The mediator once obtained the certificate can subscribe to 5 mediation agencies to perform their professional activity.

In order to become mediators, they must instead possess the following requirements:

- For theoretical courses, having published three contributions in the field of reconciliation.

- For practical courses, having carried out the activity of mediation at Accredited Bodies at Ministry of Justice, in at least 3 procedures.

- For all teachers to have completed teaching in courses mediation at Professional Orders, Entities public, national or foreign universities, as well to attend the same agencies, 16 hours update over the course of the two-year period.

The activity of the mediator falls within the scope of the media bonds because it makes use of the means to achieve the result. Such an obligation is founded on the duty of average diligence, in the right way to the level of difficulties and dangers of the activity carried out and that reflects on the level of professional diligence required.

From this comes the recognition of the compensation to the mediator regardless of the outcome of the mediation.

Among the obligations of the mediator are listed:

- impartiality

- confidentiality

- It can not play in the same dispute or the referee or defender function.

- It has the duty of information to be expressed in to make the parties aware of the legal consequences, on the effects of the conciliatory proposal on nature of the mediation that derives from activating a mediation process, mediator role.

- has the obligation to update biennial.

- has the duty to check in the contradictory that the necessary parts are present, or in them replacement representatives are provided with delegation.

- According to art. Section 14, paragraph 2 a) of the decree legislative n. 28 of 2010 the broker's job is that of subscribing to the beginning of the proceedings of mediation the declaration of impartiality in the respecting the rules of the Organization and the behavioral rules of the conciliators inspired by the deontological code approved by the UIA (Union International Attorneys' Association) in the April 2 session 2002.

From the omission are the responsibilities:

- Aquilian responsibility: neglect, imprudence, and inexperience.

- liability art. 2049 c.c.

- ex art responsibility, 2236 c.c. for breach of imperative rules and public order to which it adds also the Body's responsibility for culpa in getting out and watching for failing to check the mediator's work.

While among the rights he holds the mediator himself include:

- To ask for replacement if a justified reason, as an objective impediment.

- To appoint an experienced technical engineer particular complexity.

- By virtue of the intellectual work contract, ex. art. 2230 c.c. is entitled to an allowance and a reimbursement of expenses.

- Refrain from revealing the statement yields and information gained during the mediation.

The 23-9-2014 was published in G.U no. 221 il Decreto 4 August 2014, n. 139 Changes to D.M.180 / 2010 concerning the mediator. In particular:

- Article 14a states that the mediator does not it can be part or represent or in any way assist parties in mediation proceedings before to the body to which it is registered or to the who is a member or who carries a charge at any rate; the prohibition extends to professional members, associated or practicing in the local ones.

- Mediators who, on the date of entry into force of the the decree did not complete the update professional (assisted traineeship) referred to in art. 4, co. 3, became. b), D.M. 180/2010, are required to provide you within a period of one year from 23 September 2014[38].

---

[38] www.mondoadr.it/adr-news/vigore-il-nuovo-dm-139-che-disciplinalincompatibilit-dinteresse-conflict-of mediatori.html.

CHAPTER VIII

MEDIA BODIES, SECRETARY, EXPERTS

1. MEDIATION BODIES In D.M.180 / 2010 the mediation bodies are Public or private bodies authorized to carry out the mediation process and registered in a register held by the Ministry of Justice. The Registry is responsible for the General Manager of the civil justice exercising powers of control and supervision.

Each body has its own regulation and one ethical code to be communicated and deposited at Ministry by the act of its constitution. The requirements for constitution are:

- A capital not inferior to that of which subscription is required for the constitution of one Limited liability company;

- have an organizational capacity. The applicant must attest to be able to carry out the activity of mediation in at least two Italian regions or in at least two provinces of the same region, too through the agreements referred to in Article 7, paragraph 2, letter c);

- possession of a policy by the applicant insurance amount of not less than 500,000.00 euro for liability to any title deriving from the conduct of the mediation activity;

- Possess the integrity requirements of associates, associates, administrators or representatives of the aforesaid entities, conforming to those laid down in art. 13 of the decree Legislative February 24, 1998, no. 58;

- administrative and accounting transparency, there including the legal and economic relationship between the body and body of which it is required constitutes internal articulation at the end of demonstrating the necessary financial autonomy and functional;

- guarantees of independence, impartiality and confidentiality in the service of mediation as well as the compliance of the regulation to the law and decree 28/2010, even though concerns the legal relationship with mediators;

- the number of mediators, not less than five;

- indication of the seat of the Organization; Organizations established, even in associate form, by the CCIAA and by the advice of professional orders are registered on a simple question, on the outcome of the verification of the existence of the sole requirement of the possession of the policyholder insurance amount of not less than 500,000.00 EUR.

The enrollment order is communicated to ' Body to which an order number will be assigned in the register.

From the entry, the Organism shall communicate by 31st December March the management statement. Also, the Responsible has the cancellation of the Organizations that have done less than ten mediation procedures in a two-year period.

Cancellation prevents the Organism of get a new inscription before it's gone one year. The 23-9-2014 was published in G.U no. 221 il Decree 4 August 2014, n. 139 Changes to D.M.180 / 2010 with reference to the Organizations of mediation.

In particular:

- The bonuses paid to the Organizations regarding the start-up costs due from each side "for the first meeting ", or 80.00 euros for the disputes of worth more than 250,000 euros. It was also expressly provided that in case of failure agreement the parties must match the same amounts.

- It was expressly provided that the applicant must be guaranteed to be able to form a body a minimum capital of 10,000 euros, in lieu of "The one whose subscription is required to establishment of a limited liability company. "

- Each Entity is obliged to communicate to the Ministry at the end of each quarter, i statistical data concerning the mediation activity carried out.

- In addition to art. 10 first paragraph of the decree are provided for sanctioning provisions in the case of failure to comply with the previous provision. Indeed yes suspends, for a period of twelve months, of the Organization that did not statistical communications and / or measure of deletion from the register where the Organism itself does not send, within the next three months, the data including the "historical" of the previous twelve months;

- Mediation bodies at the date of the entry into force of the Regulation are not in possession of all the requirements of art. 4, co. 2, lett. a), D.M. 180/2010, they will have to provide for integration within 120 days. since its entry into force the same, with the cancellation penalty.

This is expressly foreseen also for the Bodies of training, with reference, of course, to requirements of art. 18, co. 2, lett. a), D.M. 180/2010[39].

2. SECRETARY

The secretariat is responsible for keeping the file of every mediation process, verifies the availability of the parties to attend the meeting, ne organizes the

---

[39] www.mondoadr.it/adr-news/vigore-il-nuovo-dm-139-che-disciplinalincompatibilit-dinteresse-conflict-of-mediatori.html

meeting, and provides communications via pec or ordinarily recommended.

3. EXPERTS

The expert is the natural person listed in the list of the Body or of the advisers of the Courts with technical expertise in certain materials.

During a complex mediation, the mediator in difficulty may apply to arrive at a better solution to the cause.

The expert participates in the mediation allowance with the appointed mediator.

CHAPTER IX

DIFFERENCES WITH ARBITRO AND IL JUDGE, DIFFERENCES BETWEEN ASSISTANCE AND MEDIA NEGOTIATION CIVIL AND COMMERCIAL

1. DIFFERENCES WITH THE ARBITRO AND IL JUDGE

Mediation differs from the referee and from the judge to be an informal procedure, in which the parts are free to run or not to the agreement reached in the latter mere contractual default.

The Referee belongs to the litigation procedure, and the its ruling (praise) on the dispute has effect binding to the parties.

The appeal to the arbitrator may be the result of a clause compromise inserted in a contract or by will of the parties by means of a different contract of Arbitrary Devolution, with the compromised name.

In Italy, two types of arbitrators are distinguished: ritual, in for which the award is as effective as a judgment pronounced by the judicial authority, in which the party the winner may apply for the execution by filing the I praise you at the court's chambers and wait for it execute by a special decree (Article 825 Code of Civil Procedure).

Irritable arbitrariness, it is when the parties, of jointly agree, they decide their dispute is defined by the referees with a gift of legal weakened effectiveness.

Upon acceptance of the assignment, the referee appointed has the obligation not to renounce the mandate received except for justified reason and to award the award within the time limit set by the parts or regulations applicable to to the proceedings. Unlike the judge, even though an organ impartial, yet its decision (judgment) binding, is intended to condemn one of the parties by applying the civil procedure.

2. DIFFERENCES BETWEEN THE TRADING CIVIL ASSISTANCE AND MEDIATION E COMMERCIAL

Assisted negotiation was introduced with D.L. 132/2014 which attributes executive effectiveness to the transactions negotiated between the parties' lawyers.

Two contracts are formed:

1) The assisted trading agreement in which all parties undertake to cooperate for one peaceful solution within a certain date.

2) The conciliation agreement that resolves the disputes under contractual clauses traded.

The remuneration for the lawyer in negotiation Assist depends on the average payout parameters lawyers.

The remuneration for the mediation body and for the mediator depend on the proportional tariffs to the value of the lite indicated in the ministerial tables. Civil mediation recognizes the right of the parties to a tax credit of up to € 500, 00.

It is exempt from stamp duty and tax register up to a value of 50.000,00 euro.

In the negotiations, the agreements signed by the spouses for the dissolution of marriage are exempt from stamp duty, registration tax, and all other taxes (Cass. No. 1145872005).

You also recognize a tax credit of 250.00 euro to those who successfully negotiate assisted.

The use of assisted negotiation is compulsory in the subjects of: compensation for vehicle traffic damage and boats

- payment of sums within 50.000,00 euro The use of mediation is mandatory in the subjects of real rights, condominium, lease, commodity, patties family, medical and health responsibility, division, inheritance succession, rent of companies, defamation, insurance contracts, banking and finanziari[40].

---

[40] www.iformediate.com

CHAPTER X

VERBAL TYPE

- The minutes of agreement, pursuant to art. 12 of the decree Legislative 28/2010, the content of which is not contrary public order or imperative rules, it is homologated, on the party's request and after the assessment also of formal regularity, with decree of the president of the court in whose district he is based the mediation body.

In cross-border disputes referred to in Article 2 of Directive 2008/52 / EC of the European Parliament and of the Council of the Council of 21 May 2008, the minutes are approved by the president of the court in which around the agreement must be executed.

The above mentioned report is an executive title for forced expropriation, for running in shape specific and for the registration of a legal mortgage.

- failure to reach agreement without formulation proposal,

- Report of non-agreement with no proposal accepted.

- minutes of non-adherence, missing minutes appearance.

CHAPTER XI

COSTS, TIMES, FREE PATROCINIO

1. COSTS

Article. 16 of D.M. 18.10.2010 n.180 in the text updated by D.M. July 6, 2011, no. 145, provides I criteria for determining the allowances due to the mediation body that includes the costs of initiating the proceedings and expenses of mediation.

On the expense of the Tar of Lazio, he had spoken with judgment no. 1351/15 of 31/1/15 on the application presented by the National Union of Chambers Civic (UNCC) of Parma against the Ministry of the Justice, Ministry of Economic Development, and it accepted the annulment of Articles 16, paragraphs 2 and 9, and 4, paragraph 3, lett. b) of Decree no. 180 of 18 October 2010 and s., Adopted by the Minister of Justice of in concert with the Minister of Economic Development. Subsequently, the State Council by Ordinance n. 1694 of April 22, 2015, in suspension partially the enforceability of the TAR judgment Lazio n. 1351/2015, stated that they are instead due to the first mediation meeting, expenses startup and documented living expenses.

Added extra and other expenses incurred for the other recommended recommendations[41].

1. TIMES

The conciliation meeting is fixed by 15 days and the whole procedure ends within 3 months from the filing date of the application.

2. FREE PATROCINIO

The discipline of free patronage is contained in the Articles. 74-145 of D.P.R. 30.5.2002, n. 115, "Text alone in respect of the costs of justice "(modified by last from l. 27.12.2013, n. 147), which sets the requirements and how to be eligible. The DPR provides, when mediation is the condition of the application of the application in question of Article 5, paragraph 1 bis, or is prepared by the judge pursuant to art. 5, paragraph 2, to the Organism no

---

[41] www.lastampa.it/dossier/settimana_conciliazione2007

allowance is due on the part that is found in the conditions for admission to patronage a state expenses, while the fee is due of the attorney who attended the party during the mediation.

The requirements to be utilized are:

- The limit of income provided for by art. 76 D.P.R. n.115 / 02 is € 11,528.41 per year.

If the person concerned lives with his / her spouse or with others family, income is the sum of the income earned in the same period by each component of the family with the only exception that you will be considering a single personal income when are the subject of the personality right, or in the processes in which the interests of the applicant they are in conflict with those of the other components family with him cohabiting.

- Being Italian or foreign citizens regularly staying on national territory at the time of the outcome of the process or of the fact being brought to light to be established or stateless or entities or associations that do not they pursue profit and do not engage in business economic.

The party concerned will have to file at the appropriate substitute declaration body of the notorious act, the subscription of which may be authenticated by the mediator, and other documents that you would be necessary.

The Organism keeps a separate register with the record of the proceedings in which there is one or several parties eligible for sponsorship at the expense of the state, on which the Ministry of Justice undertakes to carry out a control[42].

The results of such monitoring are taken into account for the determination, with the decree referred to in Article 16, paragraph 2, of the allowances to be paid to the Public bodies, so they also cover the cost of the activity carried out in favor of eligible persons exemption.

In the Annual Budget of the Organization, it deliberates about the possible breakdown of the budget in favor of those mediators who have done so

---

[42] www.lastampa.it/dossier/settimana_conciliazione2007

activities in processes where one or more parts result eligible for patronage at the expense of State.

LITE VALUE

Table A (Article 16, paragraph 4) Lite Value - Expense (for each part)

Up to Euro 1,000: Euro 65;

from Euro 1.001 to Euro 5.000: Euro 130;

from Euro 5,001 to Euro 10,000: Euro 240;

from Euro 10.001 to Euro 25.000: Euro 360;

from Euro 25,001 to Euro 50,000: Euro 600;

from Euro 50.001 to Euro 250.000: Euro 1.000;

from Euro 250.001 to Euro 500.000: Euro 2.000;

from Euro 500.001 to Euro 2.500.000: Euro 3.800;

Euro 2.500.001 Euro 5.000.000: Euro 5.200;

over Euro 5.000.000: Euro 9.200.

CHAPTER XII

NORMAL: LEGISLATIVE DECREE 28/2010, D.M. 18 OCTOBER 2010 N.180

Legislative Decree 4 March 2010, no. 28 "Implementation of Article 60 of the Law of 18 June 2009, n. 69, on finalized mediation conciliation of civil disputes and commercial "published in the Official Gazette of March 5, 2010, no. 53

THE PRESIDENT OF THE REPUBLIC

Having regard to Articles 76 and 87 of the Constitution; Given Article 60 of Law 19 June 2009, no. 69 delegating to the Government on mediation and conciliation of civil disputes and commercial;

See Directive 2008/52 / EC of the European Parliament and of the Council of 21 May 2008 on certain aspects of mediation in civil matters and commercial;

Given the preliminary deliberation of the Ministers, adopted at the meeting of 28 October 2009;

Acquire the opinions of the competent Commissions of Chamber of Deputies and Senate of the Republic;

Given the deliberation of the Council of Ministers, adopted at the meeting of 19 February 2010;

On the proposal of the Minister of Justice;

E m a n a

the following legislative decree:

Chief I

GENERAL PROVISIONS

Art. 1

definitions

1. For the purpose of this Legislative Decree, this is understood

for:

a) mediation: the activity, however named, carried out by an impartial third party and intended to assist two or more subjects in the search for an agreement friendly for the composition of a dispute, both in the formulation of a proposal for the resolution of the same;

(b) mediator: the person or natural persons who, individually or collegially, perform the mediation, while remaining devoid of power in any case to make judgments or decisions binding on I recipients of the same service;

c) conciliation: the composition of a dispute following the conduct of the mediation;

(d) body: the public or private body, at which mediation process can take place of this Decree;

(e) register: register of bodies established with decree of the Minister of Justice to the senses of Article 16 of this Decree, not only upon issuing this decree, the register of the bodies set up under the decree of the Minister of Justice 23 July 2004, no. 222.

Art. 2

Disputes mediated

1. Anyone can access mediation for the reconciliation of a civil dispute commercial property rights, according to the provisions of this Decree.

2. The this decree does not preclude negotiations voluntary and parity-related disputes civil and commercial, or complaint procedures provided by service cards.

Chapter II

OF THE MEDIATION PROCEDURE

Art. 3

Applicable discipline and form of the acts

1. The mediation procedure shall apply to the the body's governing body.

2. The Regulation must in any case guarantee the confidentiality of the proceedings under Article 9 as well as the appointment of the mediator ensure impartiality and fitness to the correct and solicitous execution of the assignment.

3. Mediation proceedings are not subject to formalities.

Mediation can take place in a mode telematics provided for in the rules of the body.

Art. 4

Access to mediation

1. The application for mediation relating to disputes referred to in Article 2 are filed by depositing an instance with an organization.

In case of multiple questions related to it controversy, mediation takes place in front to the body at which it was presented first question. To determine the time of the question is about the date of receipt of the communication.

2. The application must indicate the body, the parties, the object and the reasons for the claim.

3. When the assignment is given, the lawyer is required to inform the witness of the possibility of make use of the mediation process governed by this decree and the concessions taxation referred to in Articles 17 and 20.

The lawyer also informs the attendant of the cases in which the experiment of the mediation process and ' the legality of the proceedings.

The information must be provided clearly and for signed up. In case of violation of the information obligations, the contract between the lawyer and the attorney is void. The document containing the information is' signed by the Assistant and must be attached to the act introductory to any judgment. The judge who verifies the non - allegation of the document, if it does not provide for the purposes of Article 5 paragraph 1, informs the party of the faculty requesting the mediation.

Art. 5

Condition of processibility and relationship with the process

1. Who intends to sue a relative action?

to a dispute over the condominium, rights real, division, inheritance successions, patties family, lease, rented, rent of companies, compensation for damages arising from the circulation of vehicles and boats, medical and dental care defamation with the press or other means means of advertising, insurance contracts, banking and financial, it is supposed to be preliminarily experimented with mediation procedure under the present decree or conciliation procedure envisaged by Legislative Decree no. 179 or the procedure established in implementation of article 128-bis of the unique text of the law Banking and Credit Matters referred to in the Decree Legislative 1 September 1993, no. 385 and later modifications, for the matters governed therein. The experiment of the mediation process is' the legality of the proceedings.

The improvisability must be objected to by the defendant, at the expense of a decree, or taken office by the judge, not beyond the first hearing. The judge where you find that mediation has already begun, but it has not ended, it is fixed the next hearing after the expiry of the term of referred to in Article 6.

It also does when mediation does not she was experimenting, assigning them at the same time to the 15-day deadline for submission of the application for mediation.

This paragraph does not apply to the actions envisaged Articles 37, 140 and 140-bis of the Code of Civil Procedure consumption referred to in the Legislative Decree of 6 September 2005, n. 206, and subsequent modifications.

2. Without prejudice to paragraph 1 and save as provided for provided for in paragraphs 3 and 4, the judge, also in the place of judgment of appeal,

assessing the nature of the case, I state of education and the behavior of the parties, may invite them to mediate.

The invitation must be addressed to the parties before of the hearing to clarify the conclusions or, when such hearing is not foreseen before discussion of the case.

If the parties adhere to the invitation, the judge shall fix it subsequent hearing after the expiry of the term referred to in Article 6 and, where mediation is not already started, assigns to the parties at the same time term of 15 days for the submission of the application for mediation.

3. Mediation does not preclude in each case the grant of urgent measures and guardians, or transcripts of the application.

4. Subsections 1 and 2 do not apply:

(a) in proceedings for injunction, including the opposition, until the pronouncement on the instances of granting and suspending the provisional execution;

b) in procedures for license validation or eviction, until the change of the rite mentioned in Article 667 of the Code of Civil Procedure;

(c) in the proceedings of the holders, until the pronouncement of the measures referred to in Article 703, third paragraph, of the Civil Procedure Code;

d) in the opposition or incident proceedings of cognition regarding forced execution;

(e) in proceedings in the Chamber of Advocates;

f) in the civil action exercised in the criminal proceedings. 5. Hold as provided for in paragraph 1 and save what provided for in paragraphs 3 and 4, if the contract, the statute that is, the constitutive act of the institution provides one mediation or conciliation clause and attempt it is not experienced, the judge or the referee, by exception part, proposed in the first defense, assigns to the 15-day deadline for submission of the application for mediation and fix the next hearing after the expiry of the term

Article 6.

Likewise, the judge or arbitrator fixes it later hearing when mediation or Conciliation attempts have begun but not concluded.

The question is presented to the body indicated by the clause, if registered in the register, or, in the absence, in front of another registered body, without prejudice to the criterion set out in Article 4 paragraph 1.

In any case, the parties may agree, following the contract or the statute or the act constitutive, the identification of a different organism signed up.

6. From the moment of communication to other parties, the demand for mediation produces on the prescription the effects of the application. From the same date, the application for mediation it also prevents decadence for once, but if the attempt fails the court's application must be submitted within the same term of declines, as from the filing of the minutes of which Article 11 at the secretariat of the body.

Art. 6

Duration

1. The mediation process has a duration not more than four months.

2. The term referred to in paragraph 1 shall begin on the date of filing the application for mediation, that is from the expiry of that fixed by the court for the deposit of the same and even in cases where the court has the referral of the case to the fourth or fifth quarters period of the paragraph 1 of Article 5, is not subject to Weekly suspension.

Art. 7

Effects on the reasonable duration of the trial

1. The period referred to in Article 6 and the period for referral ordered by the court within the meaning of Article 5, paragraph 1, they are not computed for the purposes of Article 2 of Law 24 March 2001, no. 89.

Art. 8

Method

1. When submitting the application for mediation, the manager of the body designates mediator and

fixes the first meeting between non-parties more than fifteen days after filing the application.

The question and date of the first meeting are communicate to the other party with any suitable means to secure the reception, also by the party instant.

In disputes requiring specifics technical expertise, the body may appoint one or more auxiliary mediators.

2. The procedure shall be conducted without formalities at the seat of the mediation body or the place as indicated in the Rules of Procedure body.

3. The mediator works for the parties they reach a friendly definition of agreement of the dispute.

4. When it can not proceed in accordance with paragraph 1, last time, the mediator can avail himself of experts enrolled in the panel of consultants at the courts.

The body's rules of procedure must to provide for the method of calculation and liquidation of fees paid to experts.

From the lack of participation without justification reason for the mediation process the judge may to argue evidence in the next trial pursuant to the second paragraph of Article 116 of the Code of civil procedure.

Art. 9

Duty of confidentiality

1. Anyone lends their own work or their own service in the body or anyway within the framework of the Mediation procedure is required by the law confidentiality with respect to the statements made and the information obtained during the procedure same.

2. Compared to statements made and information acquired during separate sessions and save consent of the declarant or from whom the information comes, the broker is also kept confidential to the other parties.

Art. 10

Unusable and professional secrecy

1. Declarations made or information obtained during the mediation process not can be used in the trial with the same or partial object, started, summarized or continued after the failure of mediation, without the consent of the declarant or from whom information comes from. On the content of the same statements e information is not allowed testimonial evidence and no declarative oath may be deferred.

2. The mediator may not be required to defer on the content of the statements made and of the information acquired in the proceedings of mediation, in front of the judicial authority, in front of another authority. The mediator applies the Article 200 of the Code of Procedure penalties and extend the guarantees provided for the defender of the provisions of Article 103 of the Code of Criminal Procedure as applicable.

Art. 11

Conciliazione

1. If a friendly agreement is reached, the mediator forms a verbal record to which it is attached the text of the same agreement.

When the agreement is not reached, the mediator can make a proposal for conciliation. Anyhow, the mediator formulates a conciliation proposal if the parties agree to any agreement moment of the proceedings. Before the wording of the proposal, the mediator informs the parties of the possible consequences of which

Article 13.

2. The conciliation proposal shall be communicated to the parties in writing.

The parties reach the mediator in writing and within seven days, the acceptance or rejection of the proposal. In the absence of a response in the term, the proposal has been refused. Unless otherwise agreed of the parties, the proposal can not contain any reference to statements made or information acquired during the proceedings.

3. If the friendly agreement referred to in the paragraph 1 or if all parties adhere to the proposal of

```
ERROR: syntaxerror
OFFENDING COMMAND: --nostringval--

STACK:
```

www.ingramcontent.com/pod-product-compliance
Lightning Source LLC
Chambersburg PA
CBHW031922240526
45464CB00022B/639